Planning For Success
In Real Estate Sales

Your Guide To Creating

A Winning Business Plan

Matt Williams

Dedication

To my wife, best friend, and partner in everything, Beverly, I dedicate this book. Many years ago you saw something in me that I did not know existed, and over the course of our years together you have helped make me a better person. Your encouragement and belief in me when I said I wanted to leave my safe, stable, salaried job more than 30 years ago in order to try my hand at real estate sales made everything that followed possible.

I bargained with Life for a penny,
And Life would pay no more,
However I begged at evening
When I counted my scanty store

For Life is just an employer
He gives you what you ask,
But once you have set the wages
Why, you must bear the task.

I worked for a menial's hire,
Only to learn, dismayed,
That any wage I had asked of Life,
Life would have willingly paid.

-- Jessie Belle Rittenhouse (1869–1948)

Introduction

Even though we may not always be consciously aware of it, creating and following detailed plans are part of our daily lives . . . especially when we want a successful outcome. Consider these examples:

You are going on an important trip. You know when you have to leave for the airport and what time you have to arrive at the departure gate. At your destination you have reserved a car and hotel room. When you check-in you ask for a wake-up call for the next morning because you know you have several things you must do for your meeting. You leave nothing to chance because you want this to be a successful trip. You make plans. You don't 'wing it'.

You have invited some friends for a dinner party. You want the evening to be special so you thoughtfully considered where you would seat your guests, the menu, the wine, flowers, table linens, and every detail. You have even thought of some topics of conversation. You know what time you need to start preparing the dinner, and you have step-by-step recipes for each course. You develop, then follow, a plan.

You bought your daughter a bike but it came in a box and now you have to put it together. Thankfully the bike comes with a set of step-by-step instructions. Following these instructions will enable you to assemble the bike properly and in time for a Christmas morning surprise.

Plans are important to us even when we're not the ones making the plans. Imagine your child is going to have surgery. You are anxious. You meet with the doctor the night before and she explains exactly what she's going to do. She tells you who else will be in the operating room and what their roles will be. She has a plan and her preparation reassures you. Imagine how different you'd feel if you asked the doctor what she was going to do and she answered, "Oh, I don't know. I haven't really given it any thought. We'll just wing it". Would you put your child's life in the hands of someone who is just 'winging it'?

Whether you call it an itinerary, a procedure, a recipe, or a set of instructions, they all mean the same thing - a plan. Plans are tools of accomplished and successful people. There are times when freewheeling is acceptable and even desirable, but not when it comes to the effective investment of time, money, and energy as is needed to create a successful real estate career.

So why do so many agents work without a plan? Why do so many agents begin each year, month, and day with at best only a vague idea of what they want to accomplish, and more importantly, how they are going to accomplish it? Why do so many agents 'wing it'?

Ignorance may be one reason. Many agents have never been introduced to the concept of business planning, or if they have, have not been convinced of the benefits. Distraction and lack of motivation may be another. The agent may think a business plan is a good idea, but has never taken the time to create one.

Lack of leadership by the broker is certainly another possible reason. The broker may not know how to develop a plan or may not be that involved in each of his agent's businesses.

Whatever the reasons, there is no question that the vast majority of real estate agents are working without an effective plan. As a result, they are often aimless, inefficient, stressed, and earning far less than they are capable of earning. They know they can do better but they don't know how. The answer can be found in a good business plan.

I believe creating a business plan is the single most effective thing a real estate agent can do to improve his or her business. No matter what level of production the agent may be at now, creating a business plan is the first and most significant step in raising that level. And it may not be for the reason you may think.

In reality very few business plans – even well designed ones – are followed exactly. To be sure, the plan does create a roadmap and the wise agent will work to follow that roadmap. But life throws us curves (think detours and potholes) and I've yet to see an agent execute a business plan exactly as it was created.

But that isn't to say there is not great value in creating a business plan. That is because an effective plan contains three critical elements to success, each of which independently is a component of a successful venture and offers value to the agent:

1. **Goals**

2. The **Systems** you will employ to achieve the goal

3. The **Process** you will use to see that your systems are used

When an agent sits down to develop a business plan, the process demands they consider those things that are important to them. It requires extensive thought and contemplation. There are questions that must be answered. Why am I working? What is it I want to get from my labors? What do I want to accomplish in my life? What is truly important to me? The answers to these questions become our goals and our goals point us in the right direction.

Once our goals have been established, the next step is to chart a path from where the agent is now to where she wants to be (the goal). To do that we employ 'systems" - specific steps you will take, specific things you will do, to get the results you want.

Perhaps you have seen the cartoon that illustrates this point. It shows a businessman holding a briefcase standing on top of Mount Everest. The caption reads, "I was just out wandering around and I ended up here." We all know that doesn't happen. To reach the pinnacle, even if that pinnacle is your own pinnacle and doesn't have anything to do with being the best in the world, requires deliberate action.

Real estate is a business where you are paid for what you do, not what you hope for. Determining which systems you will use to achieve your goal requires you examine the effectiveness of various ways to invest your money and your time. It also requires you to look deep within yourself. It will do you no good if one of your systems involves knocking on homeowner doors if there is no way you're going to get out and knock on doors. The process of determining your systems requires you take an honest inventory of your skills and commitment.

Once you have established your goals and decided upon the systems you will use to achieve your goal, you're not done. It is not enough to have a roadmap – the roadmap must be followed. Real estate is a business that offers enormous freedom to do whatever you want each day. Human nature being what it is, we tend to shy away from those things that we would rather not do. It is much easier to go on the property tour looking at new listings than it is to talk to five strangers in order to get new clients. Deciding what you want to accomplish and creating a plan that will lead you there is worthless unless you have a means of ensuring that you stay on your path.

The business plan is like a three-legged stool. One leg is Goals, the next is Systems, and the third is a Process that ensures you stay on track. All three legs are essential. Having two without the third will leave you short of the results you desire.

I have spent nearly 30 years selling real estate, teaching real estate, and coaching real estate agents and I am amazed at how many agents do not work from a business plan. At the beginning of any given year, month, or even week, many agents have no clear idea of what they are going to do or what they need to accomplish in that year, month, or week. As a result their level of production (and income) is a reaction to events around them. They do not make things happen – things happen to them. When circumstances are good, more deals happen to them and they experience abundance. When circumstances are not good, fewer deals happen to them and they experience want. It does not have to be this way.

Certainly there are ebbs and flows to any agent's business but, and this is perhaps the most important point a real estate agent needs to grasp, success is not random. High producing agents are not high producing because they are gifted or lucky. The agents that list more, sell more, and earn more money do so because they do the right things on a more consistent basis. They are not a reaction to circumstances. They create positive circumstances, thoughtfully and deliberately. Some times are better than other times, but taken as a whole, the agent who knows what he wants to accomplish, has thoughtfully considered how he can accomplish that, and has a mechanism in place to keep him on track, will always outperform and out produce the agent who simply wings it.

The creation of the business plan requires thoughtful consideration and honesty. While it is possible for an extraordinary person to provide the questions, systems, and to ask the tough questions necessary to create an effective plan, the truth is the overwhelming majority of agents need help. That is the purpose of this book. I am going to take you through a process just as I would if you were sitting in my office and we were talking about how to make your business more effective, efficient, and lucrative. I will ask you the tough questions. I will challenge your assumptions. I will not let you fool yourself into thinking that you're going to do something that you are not going to do. The process may be new to you but in the end you will have a business plan that will have crystallized what it is you want to accomplish, the means of accomplishing it, and the method for staying on track.

In the end you will be a better agent and your business, your production, and your income will all be better. Stay with me on this. It is totally worth it.

It Starts With Goals

Why do you work? Why do you get up in the morning, shower, get dressed, go to the office, and put up with all the things real estate agents have to put up with in the course of your day? Have you ever considered the answer to this question?

For most people the answer is "To pay the bills". Life costs money and when we work we get (hopefully) the money to fund our lives. Our shelter, food, insurance, cars, education, entertainment – are all funded by our work efforts, the things we do at our jobs.

But commission real estate sales poses some unique challenges. What happens if your time and efforts on the job don't produce enough income to fund your life? It's not like a salaried job where you get the same paycheck week in and week out. What if your work doesn't provide the income you need?

Typically there are two responses - the agent leaves the real estate sales business or they scale back their lifestyle to their income level. When business is slow they cut back on going out, vacations, and saving. When business is good, there are more dinners out, elaborate vacations, and more deliveries by the UPS guy. Their lives are dependent on funding and when funding is high, life offers more opportunities. When funding is low, there are fewer opportunities.

Essentially, they adjust their lifestyle to their incomes.

That's Not How It Should Be

I want to turn that model upside down. Instead of adjusting your lifestyle to the level that your income allows, *why not adjust your income to the level needed to fund the lifestyle you want?* Why not view the reason you work as not, just to 'pay your bills', but instead, provide you the funds you need to enjoy the kind of lifestyle you want?

(Let me interject a thought at this time – work is not all about money. There are other reasons we

work [service to others and personal fulfillment are two examples of non-monetary reasons], but for most agents the primary reason they work is to earn money so they can fund their lives).

What would your life look like if you had all the money you wanted? Would you drive the same car you drive now? Would you live in the same house or apartment? Would your retirement fund look the same as it does now? How about your credit card balance?

In developing a real estate business plan we must first decide what lifestyle we want - not what we think we can have, but what we want to have.

There are two methods I use to help agents envision the life they want.

The first method is I ask them to imagine it's a year from now – exactly 365 days in the future – and we are talking about what a great year this has been. I ask them to tell me exactly what happened over the course of that year. What things happened that made it a great year? The answers might be things like, "Chris and I finally took that trip to France" or "We paid Scott's tuition without taking out a loan" or "Our retirement fund is $25,000 larger than at the beginning of the year". Whatever it is that would make their lives more like what they want it to be, we write it down.

Not every ambition needs to be grand. Playing in a golf league for the first time, going out to dinner once a month, taking dance lessons, patching the driveway – anything and everything that would make your life better, write it down.

In the second method, I ask, "Imagine you are making a movie of your life and you are the producer, the writer, the director and star of your movie. If you were not held back by any presupposed limitations, what with that movie look like"?

It is important you don't limit yourself to what you think you can do. Be bold. Step out of the shadows of your past. Make your list all you want and need. Take time to do this. Seriously consider what you need and want. This is not a list that you throw together in five minutes. You should give this careful consideration. Some agents go off on a weekend retreat to consider what they want their life to be. Be sure to include the input of those that depend on you – even your children.

Once you have made your list of wants and needs, the next step is to identify all those items on your list that you MUST have. These are the things that, if you didn't have them, would cause you to live below a level that is acceptable. The usefulness of goals to motivate you to action is only good to the extent you really want it. If you are lukewarm on some item on your initial list it is unlikely you will do what is necessary to acquire it.

Let me give you an example from a conversation I've often had. I will be talking with an agent as part of the business planning process and I ask the question, "What is it you want to accomplish from your real estate work?" Oftentimes the answer is "I want to earn $100,000." Next I ask, "What if you just made $95,000? Would that be okay with you?" If the answer is "yes", then $100,000 is not an effective goal. How could it be – you'd be satisfied even if you didn't reach it? How will you muster the energy, resilience, and persistence to achieve a goal that you are not passionate about?

For some agents a goal of $100,000 has nothing to do with their monetary needs. Instead, reaching that threshold means they have achieved a level of production they respect and is important to them. For that agent, a goal of earning $100,000 can be very effective.

What Is Your Four-Minute Mile?

For many years runners pursued the goal of running a mile in less than four minutes. There was no question what constituted success. 3:59.9 meant success, joy, and fame – 4:00.1 meant failure, disappointment, and obscurity. As the world's premier milers trained, they were passionate about that .2-second difference between accomplishment and failure. It was what spurred Roger Bannister (who was the first to break the barrier by running 3:59.4) and the others to get up early to run, adhere to a strict diet, train in all kinds of weather conditions, and make the sacrifices needed to achieve the goal.

So what is your 3:59.9 mile? What is it you are passionate about? Where is that point below which is unacceptable? Go through your list and cross out those things that, if you didn't achieve them, wouldn't bother you much.

Let's say you put down you wanted a new car. Do you really want a new car or would you just like a new car? If a year from now you were still driving the same car, would you be disturbed enough to motivate you or would you just shrug your shoulders and say "It's no big deal".

You want your list to be made up of 'big deals' – those things that, if you don't have them, will affect you in a negatively significant way. Only when we truly care about something does it then provide the power to move us.

Have you ever seen someone who is living an unfulfilled life? Many times it is because they really don't care about anything. Nothing is so important to them as to reach the level of 'passionate'. As a result, not only are they aimless, but often lethargic and undisciplined as well. However, take someone who knows what she wants and is passionate about it – who can almost taste it - and the odds are she'll marshal the energy and intellect necessary to get it.

How Much Is This Going To Cost?

From your original list you pare it down to those things that are 'must haves', things you are passionate about. The next step is to calculate what income you will need to fund this lifestyle you want. Calculating the cost of some things is easy. If you want to put aside $10,000 for retirement, you know the cost is $10,000. If your contribution to the family budget is $2000 a month, you know the number is $24,000

Other items may require a little calculation. Let's say for instance one of your goals is to go out to dinner two times a month. If you estimate $75 for each night out (including the cost of the babysitter), that means you need $150 per month or $1800 a year. Write it down.

What if you want a new car? You could put down $35,000 but it may be more reasonable to pay the car off over time with a loan. If the payment is $400 a month put down $4,800 on your goals worksheet. Do this until you have the cost for every item on your list.

For illustrative purposes let's assume you have done this, and after adding your contribution to your household budget, the amount of money you want to add to your retirement account, the cost of the Alaskan vacation you want to take, and the cost of the other items on your 'big deals' list, you determine you need $55,000 to fund the lifestyle you want. To this you add business expenses and income taxes to arrive at your Grand Number. (Your accountant can tell you your effective tax rate. If you're not sure, estimate 15% of your before tax and business expense income goal).

In our example, let's assume your tax liability is $8,500 and your business expenses are $8,000. Adding those two expenses to the $55,000 figure we need to fund the lifestyle you desire, we now know your income target is $71,500.

Let's pause for a moment and think about what this means. It means if you earn a total of $71,500, you will be able to 1) Pay your taxes, 2) Pay all your business expenses, and 3) Fund the lifestyle you want, all without incurring any debt.

Now What?

Now that you know the income level you need for the lifestyle you want, you need to translate that into real estate production. You need to calculate the number of listings, sold listings, and sales you need to realize your Grand Number. This is going to require some thought and maybe some research.

The first thing you need to do is determine your average sale price. You can rely on historical data or you can make assumptions. Let's say your average sale price is $235,000. The next step is to determine how much money you make on each closing. Because different brokers charge their clients different fees (since broker fees are negotiable), split the commission with each agent differently, and may include franchise fees or other fees, this number is going to be different for each person.

Let's assume you work for a national franchise that takes an 8% franchise fee and your broker keeps 35% of what is left, leaving you with 65%. With this information you can calculate your average commission.

The average sale price ($235,000) multiplied by your commission percentage (let's assume 3%) minus your company's franchise fee (8%) multiplied by the percentage your broker lets you keep (65%) and we now know your average commission per sale is $4,215.90. Sometimes you sell more expensive properties, other times you sell less expensive properties, but this is your average income per closing.

(There's no reason you have to base your calculations on what you have historically done. One of your focuses may be to work in a more expensive market. You decide if what you have done in the past is acceptable or if you need to work to raise your average sale price or commission fee. I've created an Excel spreadsheet that enables you to change any one of half a dozen variables so you can see the effect on your production needs. My email can be found at the back of the book. Let me know you want it and I will send it to you.)

The next step is to take our Grand Number and divide it by our average commission per sale.

Using the numbers from our example, we learn we need 17 closing sides.

So now we know if you make 17 sales you will earn enough money to pay your taxes, pay your business expenses, and fund the lifestyle you want - accomplishing all the things you listed as important to you.

We're Not Done Yet.

Now we need to allocate those 17 deals between listings sold and buyer sides. Again you can look to historical data to determine your percentage, or, if you're not happy with your current mix (for example too much of your business is with buyers), you can divide it the way you want it. Remember you are the producer, writer, director, and star of your movie (life). You decide how your business will be allocated.

For our illustration, let's assume you divide your business like many high producing agents do, making sold listings 60% of your production and sales to buyers 40%. For our example that would mean you would need 10 listings sold and 7 sales.

Despite your best efforts, not every listing sells however, so once again we look at your historical data to see what your percentage of listings taken to listings sold is. Let's assume you sell 3 out of every 4 listings you take. To get 10 to sell, you need to list 13.3 properties (rounded up to 14 - always round up).

So now you have your numbers:

Listings needed - 14

Listings that sell - 10

Buyer deals - 7

Think what this means. You now know what you have to do. You know if you list 14 houses and close on 7 buyer deals you will earn enough money to pay your taxes, pay your business expenses, and fund the lifestyle you want. This is powerful. No longer do you have to stumble in the darkness of vague (or non existent) goals never knowing if you are advancing, retreating, or standing still relative to your desires.

These numbers should be at the top of your head and in front of your eyes all the time. You should make 3 x 5 cards with these numbers on them and place them where you will see them several times during the day. Tape them to your bathroom mirror, the doorjamb leading out to your garage, the hub of your steering wheel, and your desk at work. Sear them into your subconscious mind. Make these numbers part of who you are.

Besides providing direction and motivation, these numbers should be a source of reassurance   and encouragement too. Here's why. If you need 14 listings, that means on average you must list a new property every 26 days. If you need 7 buyer deals, you need to put together a deal once every 52 days. Knowing your numbers will help offset one of the biggest challenges of being a real estate agent . . . handling disappointment.

Real estate is a business where failure happens all the time. We don't get the listing, the buyer bought a FSBO, someone we showed houses to every weekend for three months has disappeared and will not return our calls. It is not easy to remain positive in the face of so much disappointment. But if you know you need just one listing every 26 days, and one buyer deal every 52 days, you can be reassured that the string of 5, 10, or even 30 days without a success is no reason to panic or cause for thinking you can't finish the year where you want to be.

Now that we know we need 14 listings and 7 buyers, the next step is to figure out how you are going to get them. Step 1, Goals, the first leg of our stool, is complete. Now it's time to look at the second leg of our stool, Systems.

Systems

Sales and listings come from activities you undertake. You did something (mailed a postcard, hosted an open house, called a FSBO, answered the phone) that resulted in you getting a prospect who later listed their home with you or bought a home with you. These activities can be characterized as 'systems'.

A system can be thought of as a procedure or sequence of steps that result in an outcome. Some systems are simple while others can be complex. A system can exist even when we give little thought to there being any order to the steps.

When developing your business plan, the systems you want to employ are those that result in you developing new relationships with people interested in buying or selling real estate. Here's why:

The Lifecycle of a Commission Check

The end result of every successful transaction is compensation for the agent. For those employed in the real estate sales industry, getting paid is the endgame.

There is a seven step series of events that happen which results in an agent getting paid. It is helpful to understand each of the seven steps and their relationship to each other. Let's look at them in the reverse order in which they occur.

Step # 7 is the agent getting paid. You came into the office and there is a check waiting for you in your mailbox.

Step # 6 is the closing of title. The transaction between the seller and the buyer is completed.

Step # 5 is the creation of an agreement between buyer and seller. An offer is made, there is some kind of negotiation, and an agreement is reached.

Step # 4 is somewhat vague but can be thought of as "doing stuff". This all-encompassing descriptive includes everything we do for a client prior to them coming to an agreement. If we are working with the buyer, it involves researching listings, showing houses, taking offers, answering questions, etc. If we are working with the seller, it involves taking the listing, marketing the property, keeping the seller informed of market conditions, negotiating the deal, etc.

Step # 3 is getting the prospect to agree to work with us. Sometimes it is a formal contract (as with a written listing agreement), other times it's an informal "Sure, you can show us houses" form of consent.

Step # 2 involves some kind of activity that can be thought of as a presentation intended to get the prospect to consent to work with us. It can be something involved and formal such as a two hour listing presentation, or it can be something as simple as asking the question "Would you like me to show you this house?" Obviously a formal commitment is of greater value to the agent than a casual "Let's go see some houses", but the activity that results in the prospect advancing to the Step # 3 with us is Step # 2.

Step # 1 is the most important step. It is the activity that results in us coming face-to-face with a person who is interested in buying and selling real estate. It is the activity that introduces us to the people to whom we will do the presentation – however formal or informal, extravagant or simple – in an attempt to gain a working relationship. Without this step, none of the others happen.

Every deal you have ever, or will ever, close follows this process. We meet somebody, we ask if we can work for him or her, they say yes, we do stuff, we negotiate a deal, there is a closing, and we get paid. That's the process – every time. The deal may look different, but every deal follows the same pattern.

It follows therefore, if we want more of Step # 7 (getting commission checks), we have to do more of Step # 1 (getting face to face with people interested in buying and selling real estate). The more prospects an agent has the more commission checks they will get. It is for this reason the agent needs to employ systems that result in the creation of meetings with new prospects.

Years ago there was a popular Ford advertising campaign. Its message was 'Quality is Job 1'. This meant that at Ford, the most important thing was creating a quality product. More than anything else – sales, profits, community, etc. – quality was number one. For the real estate agent Job 1 is creating new relationships with people interested in buying or selling real estate.

With that in mind, here are some examples of systems that help you find prospects:

Direct Mail - You mail out letters or postcards introducing yourself or offering some kind of fair trade (for, example, I'll tell you how to improve the value of your home if you will agree to meet with me).

Open Houses – Done properly, you can meet buyers and sellers at open houses. (For an in depth look at the value of open houses, see my book, *'The 6-Figure Real Estate Agent's Guide To Hosting The Perfect Open House'*)

Sphere of Influence - The number one source of prospects for the majority of real estate agents is people they already know. Even so, most agents do little to cultivate this incredible source of business. As a result, they lose out on countless opportunities. A well thought out SOI program can generate prospects consistently year in and year out.

Expired Listings - A tried and true means of developing new relationships. Many agents make their living listing houses other agents failed to sell. If you can convince an expired listing owner to let you do a presentation, you will never lack for business.

For Sale By Owner (FSBO) Listings – This is another classic means of prospecting. An agent who's not afraid to talk to FSBOs also will never lack for business.

Informational Seminars – Though not particularly effective when you consider the cost versus its upside potential, there are some topics that can work. If you like talking in front of a crowd, seminars may be a good system for you.

Internet Advertising - Most buyers (and many sellers) start their real estate search for a home or an agent online. If you don't have a system that includes Internet advertising, you are missing out on this huge market.

Cold Calling or Door Knocking - Not many agents include this system in their plan, but I have known a few agents who have done well knocking on doors.

There are many other ways to prospect. Some are effective, others are not. What works for one agent may not work for another. There are agents who can't wait to start calling expired listings at 9 AM each morning. Other agents would rather have a root canal than call the owner of an expired listing.

In developing your business plan, there are a couple things to keep in mind as you consider which systems you will use to generate new relationships.

1. Is the system effective? Will it yield the desired result? Is it a wise investment in terms of cost versus benefit? A good way to determine effectiveness of the system is to ask yourself if you

would respond positively to your method and message if you were the prospect.

2. Is the system something you will do? It makes no sense to build a plan around cold calling, for example, if you wouldn't cold call if your life depended on it. The purpose of the business plan is not to give you a false sense of security. You may feel great knowing you have a plan that will provide you the lifestyle you want, but it is worthless if it is just words on a page.

I believe most agents can achieve their goals and certainly a six-figure income with no more than four systems. It is better to do 3 or 4 effective systems expertly than do 6 or 8 systems poorly.

Which systems you choose is mainly a matter of personal preference, but there are two that should be part of every agent's business plan – sphere of influence and direct mail.

Direct mail includes Just Listed/Just Sold postcards, random solicitations for sellers and buyers, and mailings to specific prospects. As the Internet has grown in significance, many agents have moved away from direct mail, some eliminating it completely. This is a mistake. The Internet is an extremely valuable tool for creating new relationships, however unless someone is looking specifically for an agent or property, much of the advertising on the Internet, e.g. banner ads, are just static, a hum to be ignored. A well-designed postcard offering of something of value (like the value of the home, a report on how to prepare home for sale, etc.) may also be static, but unlike the overwhelming amount of Internet static – the majority of which doesn't attract the viewer's attention – everyone looks at what arrives in his or her mailbox. They may look for just a second before throwing it away, but they do look. If your timing is right, it may lead to a call.

It is useful to know that according to the National Association of Realtors, the overwhelming majority of homeowners do not know a real estate agent. They have no idea who to contact if the need for a real estate agent arises. An attractive, professional mailer with a simple compelling message can pay huge dividends.

****

Many agents are hesitant to prospect via their friends and acquaintances - their sphere of influence. I've never understood that, unless of course their approach is so heavy-handed as to be blatantly self-serving and annoying. The truth is most agents get most of their business from people whom they know. Incredibly, this business typically finds its way to the agent, not because of, but in spite of, the agent's efforts (or lack thereof).

At a certain level I do understand an agent being uncomfortable calling their friends for business. It could come off as self-serving or even desperate. But an effective low-key approach is to put yourself in front of your friends and former clients in the form of a simple postcard, with some useful information (like a list of recent sales) 8 to 10 times a year. An alternative is you could order extra Just Sold cards and mail them to your sphere of influence database. All you want is to remind your friends that you are a real estate agent, and a successful one.

I have always looked at prospecting my sphere of influence as a duty to them. I know I will do more for them than any other agent. By actively prospecting them, I feel I am doing my part to ensure they don't end up with an agent who may not care for them as I would.

****

You want to select your systems giving careful consideration to what suits your personality and skill sets. I have a bit of a stutter when I'm rushed or nervous. I've found that cold calling is not a good fit for me. However, I enjoy meeting people face-to-face so I've done very well with open houses. You will be most effective when you are employing systems that are in line with your personality and talent.

What if you don't have the skills to implement a particular system? You have two choices: 1) get the skills, or 2) select a different system. You don't want to fool yourself by creating this wonderful business plan, full of effective systems, if you don't have the skill sets to employ them to good use. I don't think there's anything that you might want to learn that you couldn't learn if you are properly motivated, but you must be honest with yourself. This is where coaching (discussed at length later in this book) can be invaluable.

A Thought About The Costs Of Implementing Systems

Reaching the level of a high-income producer in real estate sales requires an act of faith. The old adage, "You have to spend money to make money" is certainly true in real estate sales. Agents who understand this and are willing to make investments are far more likely to succeed than agents who do not. You need to understand, however, that not every dollar spent is going to yield positive results. Some dollars will yield results, while other dollars will not. You may send out 1,000 postcards and get three listings, or you could send out 2,000 postcards and hear from no one. Unfortunately we don't know which dollar will give us the lead that results in a commission so we have to spend them all. There is only one certainty in marketing– if you don't invest in your business you will get no yield.

It is natural to want something for the money you spend, but in marketing (particularly real estate marketing) some investments offer a return sometimes, but not others. This is where you need faith. If you don't have enough faith in your system to invest in that system upfront, that system probably should not be part of your business plan.

I've Selected My Systems. Now What?

Once you have decided where to invest your time, energy, and money, the next step is to identify what action steps are needed for that system to yield results. This can be very specific or just bullet points. The important thing is that there be a roadmap for you to follow.

For example, let's say you included an expired system in your plan. Let's assume you have allocated 5 listings (of the 14 you need) with 4 of them selling next year. This means you need to list an expired listing, on average, once every 10 weeks. Here's what an Expired system may look like:

Expired System

12-month goal – 5 listings

Action Steps

1. Daily, research new expired listings. Decide which to pursue

2. Obtain Sellers phone number. If no phone number available, note address

3. Send compelling mailer

4. Follow-up with phone call

Weekly goal – 15 contacts with Expireds

Annual Cost - $750

You may also include, as part of your plan, the mailing piece you intend to use as well as the phone dialogue for follow-up. You can be as specific or detailed as you want.

Knowing what you're going to do (the steps listed) and especially the results you expect (one listing every 10 weeks) should encourage you to persevere even though positive results may not be immediately forthcoming. Sometimes the first call you make results in a listing. Other times it takes 2 months of daily discipline to get a listing. Both scenarios are OK. Too often agents give up on a system too early. Clearly identifying what is expected will help the agent overcome the temptation to ditch an effective system. Most times it's not a problem with the system but rather that the agent has unrealistic expectations and gives up on it too soon.

A good example of this is open houses. Let's say your budget includes 3 buyer deals and 2 listings from your open house system. To do this you plan to host 16 open houses in the coming year. You do the first open house and no one comes. Do you quit doing open houses? Of course not! By your own budget calculation, you will have at least 11 open houses with no positive results. Knowing this will keep you from making the costly mistake of pulling the plug on an effective system.

Here's an example of a system method for sphere of influence.

Sphere of Influence (SOI) System

Goal: 5 listings (3 of which sell). 3 buyer sides

Action Steps:

1. If not already done, prepare list of at least 200 friends, past clients, neighbors, and associates complete with mailing address, email address, phone number

2. Eight times throughout the year (January, February, March, April, May, June, September, October) mail SOI postcard.

3. Mail calendar in November

4. Reach out via phone two times during the year. The first will be in November/early December to ask if they received the calendar. The second will be in June to invite them to the Family Fun Day.

5. Set up email drip campaign that emails useful message monthly.

6. Ensure you are Facebook friends with all possible in your sphere of influence

Annual Cost - $2,000

As you develop your systems you will begin to see the need to plan ahead with the specific activities you need to do to implement your systems. For example, if you're going to send postcards to your sphere of influence, well in advance of your mailing date you have to decide on the content, produce the card, get the cards printed, addressed, and stamped.

This is where having a planning calendar pays dividends. If you know for instance, that you want to send your sphere of influence mailer on February 15, you need to backdate the production dates so the cards are ready on February 15. (A useful site I recommend is www.calendarsquick.com. For about $10/year you can download an unlimited number of useful, customizable planning calendars).

You want to have a clear and detailed System Method for each of your systems.

We now have covered two legs of our stool – goals and systems. We know what we want to accomplish and we know what we have to do. Now let's take a look at the third leg of our stool, instituting a process for staying on course.

Staying On Course

Do you know how a GPS works?

The device in your car is in constant communication with satellites that circle the earth. When you enter a destination in your GPS, a program calculates the route you need to take (your plan). As you travel, your GPS communicates with the satellites and compares your location with your plan. If you are 'on track' all is well. If you are not, it lets you know. It's a good system and a great metaphor for what a coach can do for you.

What good does it do you to have the best plan if you don't follow it? How do you profit if you know what to do but don't do it? And it's not because you're lazy. The biggest culprit in denying real estate agents of the success they might otherwise have is distractions. What kind of distractions? Well, to understand that, we need to take a look at one of the most desirable, yet destructive, aspects of the real estate sales business.

Most real estate agents are independent contractors, meaning they do not have the kind of oversight from their employer that an employee does. A broker may have a standard of production an agent must reach in order to stay in the employ of that broker, and the broker can make suggestions on how to accomplish that, but the broker can't micromanage the agent's daily activities. They can't say you have to be at work at 9 AM or you have to do an open house on Sunday. This kind of mandatory direction would qualify the agent as an employee, triggering tax consequences that neither party wants.

So the agent is free to do what he or she wants each day. That is one of the attractions of the real estate business – it's flexible. The trouble is, while it's true that an agent can go off in any direction they want each day, the reality is most directions lead to failure. Even hardworking agents are not immune to distractions or engaging in activities that will not yield good results.

This is where having an advocate for your business can be extremely valuable. What is an advocate? An advocate could be broker or sales manager, a coach that you hire, or even a really good friend who knows the real estate business and cares about you enough to tell you the truth. What you're looking for is someone to be accountable to. Someone you tell what activities you are going to do, and then later, whether you did them or not.

It is possible you could be your own "accountability partner". Many agents are extremely disciplined and capable of charting their course each week and then measuring their performance against that plan. So it doesn't have to be someone else.

The extra value in having a coach is that a coach will not only hold you accountable, but also work to bring the best out in you. He will ask the tough questions. He will help develop the skills you may need to improve in order to reach your goals. A coach can pick you up when you're down. A coach can help you keep things in their proper perspective. A good coach can help guide you to success.

This illustration may help you better understand the value of a coach:

I once took my daughter to the horse races. In one race, a beautiful 3-year-old mare named *Run to Mama* took two strides out of the gate, stumbled, and then threw her rider to the ground. We watched closely to see what would happen next.

As the rest of the horses raced down the backstretch, *Run to Mama* set off after them, albeit riderless. It was sad to see. Born to run and full of desire, the horse clearly knew what it was supposed to do . . . run. But without a jockey to guide and encourage her, Run to Mama fell further and further behind.

Not only that, but she was aimless. As the rest of the field stormed past our trackside viewing position, *Run To Mama* was just coming into the homestretch. And she wasn't even running on the rail, the shortest distance. She was running in the middle, then drifting towards the outer rail, looking up at the crowd. She finished 30 lengths behind.

What a beautiful, powerful animal, but what a waste, because she didn't have someone to direct, inspire, and channel that magnificent talent into a great result.

I think many agents are like that riderless horse. They may know what they are supposed to do. They may want to do what they are supposed to do. And they put out a great effort. But without someone to set them on the right path, keep them on the right path, and encourage and inspire them to do their best, they do far less than they are capable of doing.

Even the greatest talents need help in charting a course, staying on that course, and getting the most out of all their talent. That is the value a coach can provide.

These are the qualities you should look for in a coach:

1. You must respect your coach. If you don't believe your coach knows what he is talking about, there is no reason to waste your time and money. You want to know that your coach has done what he's asking you to do. You want to know that your coach

understands the challenges you have intimately. You want to have confidence in the person you trust to keep you on track.

2. You must believe your coach has your best interests at heart. You need to know your coach cares about you and your success.

3. Your coach must be available when you need him. Coaching is not just holding someone accountable, it also is providing solutions to the many problems that real estate agents face seven days week. A good coach understands that the phone call he gets on Sunday afternoon from the agent unsure of how to handle a problem, not only solves the problem this time, but every time it comes up in the future. That makes for a stronger agent.

Great actors have acting coaches. Great golfers have golf coaches. Opera singers have voice coaches. No one ever said you are expected to do this on your own. A capable, caring, accessible coach is worth tens of thousands of dollars to a dedicated agent. The ideal situation is to find that coach within your own organization, but if you cannot, you should consider hiring one of many coaches that specialize in real estate. A few hundred dollars a month may amount to less than one sale. If your coach helps you close three or four more sales a year, the return on investment is well worth it. Just build the cost into your budget.

A Final Word

Several years ago I wrote an article for Realtor Magazine entitled "Why New Agents Fail". I identified four reasons that play a part in more than 3 out of 4 agents leaving the real estate sales business even before it's time to renew their license once.

One of the reasons was the barrier to entry into the real estate business is very low. Pass a course, pass the state exam, and find a broker who will hold your license and you are a real estate agent. But being a real estate agent and being a real estate agent who makes her living and funds her life in the way she wants are two very different things. Successful agents know how to properly invest their time, efforts, and money. The effective utilization of resources requires a well-conceived plan. Every, and I mean every without exception, successful business operates from some kind of plan. Do you know why the overwhelming majority of businesses fail? Do you know why the overwhelming majority of real estate agents fail – or if not fail, live far below the standard of living they desire? It is because they have planned to fail by failing to identify their goals, methods, and means to implement those methods . . . in other words, a plan.

I hope this book has convinced you of a couple things:

1. If you want the greatest return on your investment of time, energy, and money, your likelihood for success is significantly higher if you take the time to think about what you want to accomplish, how you're going to accomplish it, and how you will combat distractions.

2. The creation of an effective business plan does not have to be painful or even time-consuming. Many very good business plans are put together in just a few hours. Once you have refined your plan – eliminating those systems that don't yield the results you want, and adding systems that do – modifying the plan each year is a relatively simple task – largely centered around your goals and what it is you want to accomplish.

It saddens me to see good agents, agents who desire a better quality of life, agents who are capable of living a better quality of life, resign themselves to lives of want when abundance is within their reach. A business plan comprised of goals, effective systems, and a method for staying on course helps free the talent and potential that is in each one of us.

I wish you the best!

About The Author

Matt Williams started his real estate career as a part-time agent in 1986 with a small independent company. He learned to sell real estate by reading books, watching others and making mistakes. He counts Floyd Wickman as a friend and mentor and credits him with making the biggest impact on his career.

After an award-winning sales career, he became a manager for one of the nation's largest independent companies. In 2002 he opened his own company, Realty Executives – Williams-Sykes Realty in the Hudson Valley region of New York.

The agents with his company have closed more transactions per agent than every other company in his marketplace every year since 2006.

www.ingramcontent.com/pod-product-compliance
Lightning Source LLC
Chambersburg PA
CBHW070945180526
45168CB00003B/1170